Greetings From Charleston

FRANCIS MARION HOTEL, CHARLESTON, S. C.—41

Elks Club, Charleston, S. C.

Mary Martin and Nathaniel Wolfgang-Price

Schiffer Publishing Ltd®

4880 Lower Valley Road, Atglen, PA 19310 USA

Acknowledgments

To John Duncan for his tireless efforts to fact check. He is a fine historian, and notable Native Son. He and his wife, Virginia, operate V & J Duncan Antique Maps, Prints & Books in Savannah.

Published by Schiffer Publishing Ltd.
4880 Lower Valley Road
Atglen, PA 19310
Phone: (610) 593-1777; Fax: (610) 593-2002
E-mail: Info@schifferbooks.com

For the largest selection of fine reference books on this and related subjects, please visit our web site at **www.schifferbooks.com**
We are always looking for people to write books on new and related subjects. If you have an idea for a book please contact us at the above address.

This book may be purchased from the publisher.
Include $3.95 for shipping.
Please try your bookstore first.
You may write for a free catalog.

In Europe, Schiffer books are distributed by
Bushwood Books
6 Marksbury Ave.
Kew Gardens
Surrey TW9 4JF England
Phone: 44 (0) 20 8392-8585; Fax: 44 (0) 20 8392-9876
E-mail: info@bushwoodbooks.co.uk
Website: www.bushwoodbooks.co.uk
Free postage in the U.K., Europe; air mail at cost.

Copyright © 2006 by Schiffer Publishing, Ltd.
Library of Congress Control Number: 2006921734

All rights reserved. No part of this work may be reproduced or used in any form or by any means—graphic, electronic, or mechanical, including photocopying or information storage and retrieval systems—without written permission from the publisher.
The scanning, uploading and distribution of this book or any part thereof via the Internet or via any other means without the permission of the publisher is illegal and punishable by law. Please purchase only authorized editions and do not participate in or encourage the electronic piracy of copyrighted materials.
"Schiffer," "Schiffer Publishing Ltd. & Design," and the "Design of pen and ink well" are registered trademarks of Schiffer Publishing Ltd.

Designed by Mark David Bowyer
Type set in Americana XBd BT / Souvenir Lt BT

ISBN: 0-7643-2488-8
Printed in China
1 2 3 4

Contents

The Simonton Gateway, Charleston, S. C.—29

Preface

By John Duncan

Born at Baker Hospital and a twelfth generation Charlestonian, I grew up in St. Andrews Parish west of the Ashley River practically next door to the public school. I always remember visiting relatives on Tradd, Montague, and Legare Streets. But it was the music lessons on Meeting Street and art classes at the Gibbes Art Gallery and attending performances at the Dock Street Theatre that instilled in me a love of Charleston and local history. As a 1959 graduate of the College of Charleston, I remember buying a stack of old Charleston postcards from either Mr. Peacock or Mr. Ziegler at their Book Basement shop on the edge of the campus. Fifty years ago I bought new Charleston postcards available at Kress and Silver's at five cents each. Art postcards like those by Elizabeth O'Neil Verner were more expensive at speciality shops. After receiving a masters degree from the University of South Carolina and a doctorate from Emory, I followed an old Charleston tradition and moved to Savannah. For thirty-two years I taught history at Armstrong Atlantic State University where my most popular course was local history. Indeed when you stop and think about it, all history is local history and what better way to enjoy it than through old postcards.

Introduction

Simply put, Charleston is a beautiful and historic city. With its location on a peninsula between the Ashley and Cooper Rivers on the edge of the Atlantic Ocean, its temperate climate, distinctive architecture and gracious lifestyle, it is easy to understand Charleston's popularity with tourists from this country and abroad.

Charleston had its beginning back in the 1660s, as one of the original thirteen colonies settled by the British in what would later become the United States of America. Even before the Revolutionary War, Charleston's port location and prosperous plantations produced a city steeped in culture, sophistication, and material wealth. The glitter of the city and its inhabitants fascinated those who came and inspired many more people to visit.

Even after the devastation caused by the Civil War and two subsequent natural disasters, people still came to Charleston to view the faded mansions of former plantation owners, bask in the warm climate, bathe at the shores, and to experience the history that was still fresh in so many minds. Where visitors went postcards followed and soon they were being sent from Charleston to cities and towns across the country and the world by tourists anxious to "drop a line home." Postcards from the 1900s to the 1950s, showcase some of the remarkable highlights of the "Palmetto City." Quoted material from the back of the cards is included in the captions along with historical trivia and present day facts.

P. A. 12569a. Charleston S. C. from St. Michaels Church, Charleston, S. C.

Charleston, South Carolina as seen from the spire of St. Michael's Church on Meeting Street.

Circa 1910s, $9-11

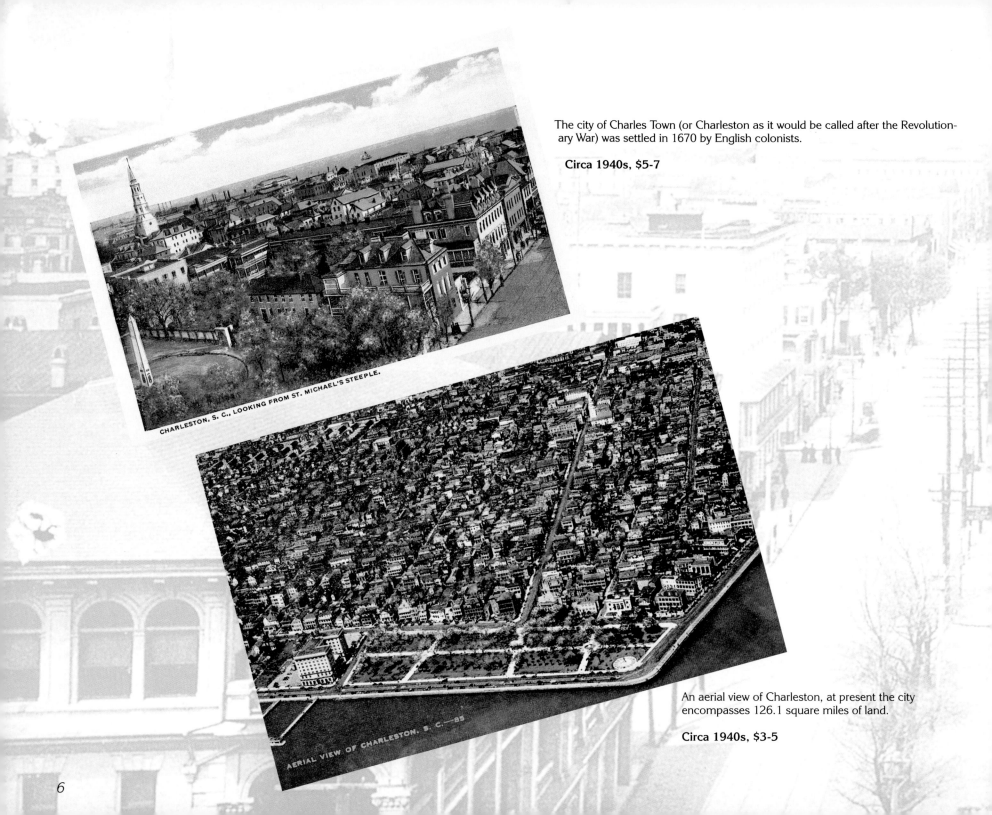

The city of Charles Town (or Charleston as it would be called after the Revolutionary War) was settled in 1670 by English colonists.

Circa 1940s, $5-7

CHARLESTON, S. C., LOOKING FROM ST. MICHAEL'S STEEPLE.

AERIAL VIEW OF CHARLESTON, S. C.—85

An aerial view of Charleston, at present the city encompasses 126.1 square miles of land.

Circa 1940s, $3-5

BIRD'S EYE VIEW OF CHARLESTON, S. C.

The name "Charles Town" was in honor of England's King Charles II.

Circa 1910s, $4-6

C.T. 31—View from Francis Marion Hotel, Looking towards Cooper River Bridge, Charleston, S. C.

3727-29-N

Looking from the top of the Francis Marion Hotel, a number of historic Charleston landmarks like the old Citadel, the Calhoun Monument, First Baptist Church, and the old Cooper River Bridge are visible.

Circa 1930s, $4-6

A "b.e.v." (bird's-eye view) of Charleston looking east.

Circa 1900s, $6-8

B. E. V. of Charleston, S. C.
Looking East.

Ten years after the colony's founding, Charleston moved from its original spot on the west bank of the Ashley River to its current location on Oyster Point in 1680.

Circa 1900s, $6-8

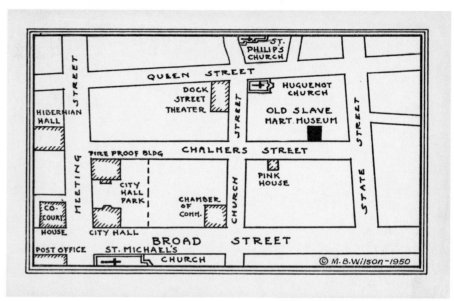

A map of a section of Charleston highlights the important buildings found on Meeting, Broad, Church, Chalmers, and Queen Streets.

Circa 1950s, $3-5

In 1850, Charleston was the South's second largest city with a population of 42,985.

Circa 1900s, $6-8

C. T. 16—Aerial View of the Citadel, Charleston, S. C.

OB-H1209

An aerial view of the Citadel, the Military College of South Carolina. The school was established in 1842 as a "school of arts and arms."

Circa 1940s, $4-6

BIRD'S-EYE VIEW OF HARBOR, CHARLESTON, S. C.

A bird's-eye view of the waterfront and Charleston Harbor.

Circa 1930s, $5-7

History

In 1663, the newly restored King of England ,Charles II, granted all lands from thirty-one to thirty-six degrees north latitude and extending west towards the Pacific Ocean to eight of his friends and closest supporters. A charter was issued on March 24, 1663 giving them the land and naming all eight Lords Proprietors of Carolina.

The colony was established in l670 by settlers from England and Barbados. The town was called Charles Town to honor King Charles II.

Ten years after the first landing, the town was moved from the west bank of the Ashley River across and down the river to its current location on Oyster Point. From there the city of Charleston as it is known today began to develop. Trade flourished with indigo, deerskins, and rice being the primary exports and manufactured goods and luxury items being the primary imports. Charleston also housed a thriving slave trade dealing in African and Native American slaves.

Eventually, South Carolina joined the other colonies in rebellion by adopting a state constitution on March 26, 1776 months before the Declaration of Independence on July 4 of that same year. Charleston was attacked twice during the Revolutionary War and was finally occupied by British forces in 1780 who remained in the city until they retreated in 1782. After the Revolutionary War, the name of the city was officially changed to the current spelling of Charleston symbolically severing any ties the city might have had with Great Britain.

Charleston continued to prosper after the Revolution and the invention of the cotton gin in 1793 added the lucrative cash crop of cotton to the list of Charleston's exports. Unfortunately with cotton came plantations, and with plantations came an increased demand for slave laborers. As the capital of Southern slavery, Charleston stood to lose the most should the institution be abolished and the almost continuous attacks by Northern abolitionists beginning about 1830 did nothing to improve the citizens' attitudes toward the concept of emancipation.

For years the battle over slavery, individual rights and states rights raged on everywhere from the halls of the national government to the parlors of private homes. Finally in a move it was thought would resolve the issue once and for all, Charleston hosted a Secession Convention on December 18, 1860. Two days later the state voted to secede from the Union and signed an Ordinance of Secession that same night. On April 12, 1861, approximately four months after the Ordinance, the first shots of the American Civil War were fired at Union troops at Fort Sumter from Confederate batteries at Mt Pleasant, and on James, Sullivan's and Morris Islands.

Despite the hardship imposed by a Union blockade, Charleston moved into Civil War with its spirit undaunted and its fervor undiminished. During the course of the Civil War Charleston was repeatedly attacked from both land and sea. Finally in 1863, Union soldiers captured Morris Island and then commenced a spectacular bombardment upon Fort Sumter. A bombardment of the city was begun in August of that year. After General Sherman's famous 1864 March to the Sea, Charleston was cut off from the rest of the Confederacy by land and by sea. In 1865, Charleston was abandoned by the Confederate Army and on February 17, 1865 Fort Sumter fell. The city was occupied by the Union Army a day later.

Charleston endured Reconstruction in a much more subdued spirit. Politics, the economy, and the very way of life for Charleston had been placed in disarray with the state government doing little to help. Cotton was still King but few planters had enough money to hire laborers. A system of tenant farming, sharecropping, and shrewd money management made some planters prosperous but nowhere near the level of antebellum years. New industries like textile manufacturing brought back a measure of prosperity and Charleston began on the road to economic and social recovery. A number of prominent public buildings and institutions were established during this time period. Despite extensive damage caused by the earthquake of 1886 and a hurricane in 1895, Charleston continued to move on and rebuild, helped by the enthusiasm and civic pride of recent immigrants and native Charlestonians. The tourist trade also became very popular with hundreds of visitors coming to Charleston to tour the historic spots and enjoy the pleasant climate. Today Charleston is a prosperous city once again with thriving tourist, manufacturing, and shipping industries as well as many beautiful and historic buildings.

SLAVE QUARTERS ON PLANTATION NEAR CHARLESTON, S. C.   —Photo by Bayard Wooten

Old slave quarters on a plantation near Charleston. The city had a sizable African-American population numbering 22,973 just before the Civil War.

Circa 1930s, $5-7

Since they could not expand in the front or back, many older Charleston houses had side piazzas in place of front or back yards.

Cancelled 1943, $6-8

SIDE PIAZZAS   CHARLESTON, S. C.

DRAWN BY ELIZABETH O'NEILL VERNER
38 TRADD STREET

11

WAITING FOR THE BUS   CHARLESTON, S. C.

DRAWN BY ELIZABETH O'NEILL VERNER
38 TRADD STREET

One of Charleston's famous flower sellers. "Highly competitive aggressive sellers," they tended to congregate below Broad Street. Carrying baskets on their heads, was a typical practice in the city and throughout the Carolina Low Country.

Circa 1940s, $4-6

Waiting for a bus, Charlestonians gather around a wrought-iron gate and fence.

Cancelled 1951, $6-8

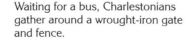

"Just as the Sword Gate in Charleston sets the style in iron gate design so also 'In Charleston It's Henry's for fine food.'"

Circa 1940s, $4-6

Fort Sumter

The plans for Fort Sumter came out of the War of 1812. President James Madison decided that more modern and therefore more effective defensive fortifications should be built along the United States coast. In Charleston Harbor, Army engineers chose a shoal projecting from James Island called the Middle Ground. Located in the middle of the harbor entrance, it was the ideal location for a new harbor fort. The fort was named Fort Sumter in honor of Revolutionary War General, Thomas Sumter.

Construction of the fort was begun in 1828 but was excruciatingly slow. An unskilled workforce, a shortage of available materials, intolerable heat in the spring and summer months, mosquitoes, yellow fever, a legal dispute as to the ownership of the property where the fort was going to be built, and the constant disruption of the tides all contributed to the slow pace of the fort's construction. By 1860, the fort was still uncompleted with only fifteen of the 135 proposed guns mounted and the officers quarters and barracks still under construction.

Despite its unfinished state, Fort Sumter came to the nation's attention on April 12, 1861 when the first shots of the Civil War were fired at the fort by Confederate batteries. In late December 1860, Major Robert Anderson moved his two small companies of the 1st U.S. Artillery from Fort Moultrie on Sullivan's Island to the more defensible Fort Sumter. Calls by Confederate authorities for the garrison to surrender were ignored and attempts to resupply the fort and reinforce the garrison were repelled. Word reached the Confederate authorities that a relief fleet was on its way to Fort Sumter. Unwilling to let the fort be resupplied and reinforced, they gave permission to Brigadier General P.G.T. Beauregard to fire on the fort if a surrender was not given by the Federal garrison. Major Anderson refused, and at 4:30 am on April 12, 1861 Confederate batteries on James, Sullivan's, and Morris Islands, and Mt. Pleasant opened fire on Fort Sumter and continued their bombardment until April 14, when Major Anderson surrendered. Despite the ferocity of the barrage there were no fatalities on either side and only five injured. Fort Sumter remained in Confederate hands until it was evacuated in 1865. Over the years Fort Sumter has seen sporadic use and was finally made a National Monument in 1948 and currently serves as one of Charleston's more popular tourist attractions.

OLD GUN POSITIONS, FORT SUMTER, CHARLESTON, S. C.   111668

The old gun positions on Fort Sumter. Despite vicious shelling for three days, there were no fatalities on either side.

Circa 1940s, $3-5

FORT SUMTER, CHARLESTON HARBOR, CHARLESTON, S. C.

Fort Sumter was built after the war of 1812 as one in a series of forts protecting vital areas along the southern coast of the United States.

Circa 1940s, $4-6

The fort was named after Revolutionary War General Thomas Sumter nicknamed "The Gamecock" for his fearlessness and fierceness in battle.

Circa 1900s, $5-7

1605—Fort Sumter, Charleston Harbor, Charleston, S. C.,

Fort Sumter–Charleston, S.C.

At 4:30 am on April 12, Confederate troops began firing on Fort Sumter and the Federal troops stationed there. A mortar shot from Fort Johnson on James Island was the first shot in the conflict and consequently the first shot fired in the Civil War.

Circa 1910s, $7-9

Views of Fort Sumter before and after the Confederate bombardment. After the capture of the fort in 1861 it was garrisoned by Confederate troops until 1865.

Circa 1900s, $6-8

FORT SUMTER, BEFORE AND AFTER THE BOMBARDMENT.   CHARLESTON, S. C.

HAND-COLORED

Fort Moultrie

Fort Moultrie was the name given to a series of forts that stood on Sullivan's Island in Charleston Harbor. The first fort built there was made from soft palmetto logs. During the Revolutionary War it was this fort that withstood a bombardment from a squadron of British warships under the command of Admiral Sir Peter Parker. According to local legend, the walls of the fort did not crack or break under the barrage. During the bombardment Sergeant William Jasper, at great risk to his own life, leapt over the parapet of the fort and replaced the South Carolina flag that had been cut down by a British cannonball, an act which earned him a place in Southern and national history.

The British, unable to destroy the fort or land any troops gave up the attack and left. The fort was later named Fort Moultrie in honor of Colonel William Moultrie who had commanded the fort during the British attack. Because of his role in the defense of the fort and of Charleston, William Moultrie was promoted to brigadier general and the image of the palmetto was added to the South Carolina flag. Francis Marion, who later distinguished himself in guerilla warfare against the British also served at Fort Moultrie.

After the Revolutionary War, a new fort was built over the remains of the first Fort Moultrie in 1798 as part of a systematic fortification of important harbors along the U.S. coast. The second fort was destroyed by a hurricane in 1804 and a more modern brick fort was constructed in 1809.

Fort Moultrie continued to play an important role in the history of Charleston. Federal troops stationed at Fort Moultrie evacuated to the more defensible Fort Sumter in 1860 after South Carolina seceded from the Union. The fort remained in Confederate hands until it was abandoned in 1865. In the 1870s and '80s the fort was modernized and made part of a larger military complex. Recently, Fort Moultrie was turned over to the National Park Service, which operates it as a national park and historic site.

Post Chapel. Fort Moultrie. Charleston. S. C.   T29

The Post Chapel at Fort Moultrie, until 1947 the fort was maintained as an active military post.

Circa 1940s, $4-6

ENTRANCE TO FORT MOULTRIE, SULLIVAN'S ISLAND, NEAR CHARLESTON, S. C.

The entrance to Fort Moultrie, the view shows some of the old cannons used in the bombardment of Fort Sumter.

1940s, $3-5

Fort Moultrie, from which the first gun was fired that started the Civil War April 13, 1860, Charleston, S. C.

The original structure of Fort Moultrie was made from palmetto logs, that according to legend, did not crack or split open during the bombardment from British warships. The fort was later named after its commander Colonel William Moultrie.

Circa 1900s, $3-5

Fort Moultrie and Grave of Osceola, Charleston, S. C.

The interior of Fort Moultrie, showing the grave of Osceola, the noted Seminole warrior and leader who died at Fort Moultrie.

Circa 1910s, $3-5

The Battery

Battery Park, or the Battery as locals say, is located on the shores of the Cooper and Ashley Rivers on the tip of the Charleston peninsula. The area was originally called White or Oyster Point because of the piles of bleached oyster shells that accumulated there. During the eighteenth century rocks and other heavy materials were used to reinforce the edge of the peninsula along the Cooper River to help control flooding caused by storms and high tides.

As the city grew the area developed and grew into the Battery. In 1837, it was used as a public park. During the Civil War, it was used as an artillery emplacement. It offers the best view of Fort Sumter and it was here that the citizens of Charleston came to watch the first bombardment of Fort Sumter and the other naval battles that took place in Charleston Harbor. Currently, the Battery is home to a number of historic residences and a public park, White Point Gardens.

An affluent part of the city, the Battery is home to many beautiful and historic homes.

Circa 1910s, $5-7

The guns along the East Battery. These guns and others like them played an important role in the defense of Charleston during the Civil War.

Cancelled 1902, $4-6

EAST BATTERY, CHARLESTON, S. C.—59

A view of the East Battery and the Fort Sumter Monument. Fort Sumter and other historic fortifications in Charleston Harbor can be seen from this spot.

Circa 1930s, $3-5

South Battery, showing Villa Margherita, Charleston, S. C.—23

The South Battery and Villa Margherita.

Circa 1900s, $5-7

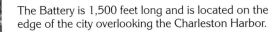

South Battery, Charleston, S. C.

The Battery is 1,500 feet long and is located on the edge of the city overlooking the Charleston Harbor.

Circa 1900s, $4-6

C. T. 4—Point of Battery and Statue,
Showing Junction of Ashley and Cooper Rivers, Charleston, S. C.

The southeastern corner of the Battery,
showing the junction of the Ashley and
Cooper Rivers. Also pictured is one of the
cannons salvaged from the Union ironclad
Keokuk.

Circa 1940s, $3-5

SCENE AT THE BATTERY, CHARLESTON, S. C.—70

One of the palmetto trees found in Battery Park. One of
Charleston's official nicknames is the "Palmetto City"
and some Charlestonians say "Palmetto Sunday" not
Palm Sunday.

Circa 1940s, $3-5

Copyright 1905 by the Rotograph Co.
G 12569 South Battery Park, Charleston, S. C.

A pair of Civil War mortars
guard one of the entrances to
South Battery Park.

Cancelled 1906, $3-5

20

Another view of Battery Park, this one showing the monument dedicated to Revolutionary War hero, Sergeant William Jasper.

Circa 1910s, $4-6

The sunset along the Ashley River, as seen from Battery Park.

Cancelled 1950, $4-6

Located at the tip of the Battery, White Point gardens has been a public park since 1837.

Circa 1930s, $4-6

Monuments and Memorials

Over the years a number of significant events have occurred in Charleston and a number of famous people have called the city home. To commemorate these events and honor those people, a number of monuments and memorials have been erected around the city.

One of the first monuments erected in Charleston was a marble statue of William Pitt the Elder, Earl of Chatham and Prime Minister of England from 1766-68. It was he who was instrumental in helping to repeal the hated Stamp Act of 1765. In recent years it was moved inside to protect it from further deterioration. Others include the small section of Charleston's old siege wall, a granite column and statue dedicated to statesman John C. Calhoun, a bronze statue dedicated to Revolutionary War hero Sergeant William Jasper, and a monument on the East Battery to the Confederate defenders of Fort Sumter.

CHARLESTON, S.C. - OLD SIEGE WALL, MARION SQUARE

This small bit of tabby in Marion Square is all that remains of the fortifications built by the Continental Army to defend Charleston during the Revolutionary War.

Circa 1900s, $4-6

Monument in Washington Square dedicated to native Charlestonian Henry Timrod, known as the "Poet Laureate of the Confederacy."

Circa 1910s, $4-6

This memorial in St. Phillip's Churchyard is dedicated to John C. Calhoun, the well-known Charleston politician who served as a United States Senator from 1832-43 and again from 1845-50. He was also vice-president under Andrew Jackson and an outspoken defender of slavery and states rights.

Circa 1900s, $3-5

Jasper Monument, CHARLESTON, S. C.

Monument dedicated to Sergeant William Jasper, who during the bombardment of Fort Moultrie risked his life under heavy British fire to replace a South Carolinian flag that had been shot down.

Circa 1900s, $4-6

Located in Middleton Place Gardens, this mausoleum contains the remains of Arthur Middleton, one of the South Carolina signers of the Declaration of Independence.

Circa 1910s, $3-5

Osceola was the Indian leader during the Second Seminole War. His grave is located in Fort Moultrie where he died three months after his capture in 1838.

Circa 1900s, $3-5

Located on the East Battery the Fort Sumter Memorial is dedicated "To the Confederate defenders of Charleston. Fort Sumter – 1861-65" and stands facing Fort Sumter.

Circa 1940s, $4-6

The Historic Pitt Monument (The Arms of this figure were shot off by the British during the Siege of Charleston, 1780), Charleston, S. C.

The South Carolina Commons House voted in 1766 to erect this marble statue of English Prime Minister William Pitt the Elder, in appreciation for the minister's efforts in repealing the Stamp Act. For protection this weathered statue has been moved in recent years to the Charleston Museum.

Circa 1900s, $4-6

Calhoun Monument, Charleston, S. C.

Buried underneath the cornerstone of the monument are a number of items including a lock of Calhoun's hair, and a copy of the last speech he delivered in the United States Senate.

Circa 1920s, $4-6

Calhoun Monument, showing Citadel, Charleston, S. C.

Erected in honor of politician John C. Calhoun, this monument is eighty feet tall and was completed in 1896.

Circa 1900s, $3-5

Cemeteries

Associated with unpleasant concepts and superstitions cemeteries are not often seen as a major tourist attraction in any city. However, it bears noting that a number of old cemeteries hold as much history as any city museum or library. Charleston's Magnolia Cemetery is the final resting place of a number of prominent citizens, including the fierce secessionist, Barnwell Rhett. Civil War soldiers and veterans like the crew of the *H.L. Hunley* (the first submarine to sink an enemy vessel) rest here as well as a number of cultural and political figures. Besides Magnolia Cemetery, Charleston was home to a number of private and church cemeteries including the St. Phillip's and St. Michael's Episcopal churchyards where a number of famous locals are also buried. In fact many Charlestonians believe that to be buried in the shadow of St. Michael's is almost as good as being alive anywhere else.

Charleston, S. C. Along the Eastern driveway, Magnolia Cemetery showing Obelisk.

A view of Magnolia Cemetery along the eastern driveway in the cemetery. The obelisk is one of many impressive memorials found throughout the grounds.

Circa 1900s, $3-5

One of the many live oaks that can be found inside Magnolia Cemetery.

Circa 1910s, $2-4

The old oak tree in Magnolia Cemetery is one of the oldest trees in the state and is said to be over a thousand years old.

Circa 1910s, $3-5

CHARLESTON, S. C. - OLD OAK TREE, MAGNOLIA CEMETERY.

Magnolia Cemetery was established around 1850 and is the burial place of a number of famous and socially prominent Charlestonians as well as a number of Civil War soldiers and veterans.

Circa 1910s, $3-5

1609—Magnolia Cemetery, Charleston, S. C. *The Comanche is not so modern as the Apache but rides full as steadily because not so top heavy. Wish you were all here.*

Scene in National Cemetery, Charleston, S. C.

The National Cemetery outside of Charleston, South Carolina. Most of the graves in the cemetery are for military personnel and their spouses.

Cancelled 1916, $3-5

Streets and Squares

The first street plan for the colony of Charles Town was devised in the 1680s by the Lords Proprietors and mapped out by local surveyors, imposing a rather rigid grip in the irregular and watery land of Oyster Point. The plan incorporated what would later become East Bay, King, Meeting, and Church streets and divided the city into immense city blocks with six hundred feet per side. The plan did not last long however, and settlers soon took the city design into their own hands breaking up the grid into more convenient streets, filling in creeks and streams, and making new roads as the town outgrew its original limits giving the city plan an irregular quality fraught with dead-ends and one way streets that confound visitors to this very day.

Because of the buildings located there, the intersection of Broad and Meeting Streets is known as the Corner of Four Laws. St. Michael's Church represents the Law of God, Charleston City Hall represents the Law of the City, the County Courthouse represents, the Law of the State, and the Post Office represents the Law of the Country.

Circa 1940s, $4-6

A view of Marion Square located near the center of the city, showing the old Citadel and the Calhoun Monument.

Circa 1900s, $4-6

Charleston, S. C. Washington Square.
4544.

Behind City Hall, Washington Square is home to several monuments.

Cancelled 1907, $4-6

WASHINGTON SQUARE, SHOWING W. L. I. PITT AND TIMROD MONUMENTS, CITY HALL, AND ST. MICHAEL'S CHURCH, CHARLESTON, S.C.

Another view of Washington Square showing City Hall and the Spire of St. Michael's Church in the background.

Circa 1900s, $5-7

CHARLESTON, S.C.-KING STREET.

King Street, most the city's retail business was transacted here.

Circa 1900s, $6-8

A view of King Street looking north.

Circa 1920s, $6-8

King Street was the retail center of Charleston. "The best stores are located where the picture was taken."

Circa 1910s, $5-7

Besides shops, King Street was home to a number of other points of interest including the Pringle House, and the house of Charles Frazer, the well-known miniature portrait painter.

Circa 1940s, $6-8

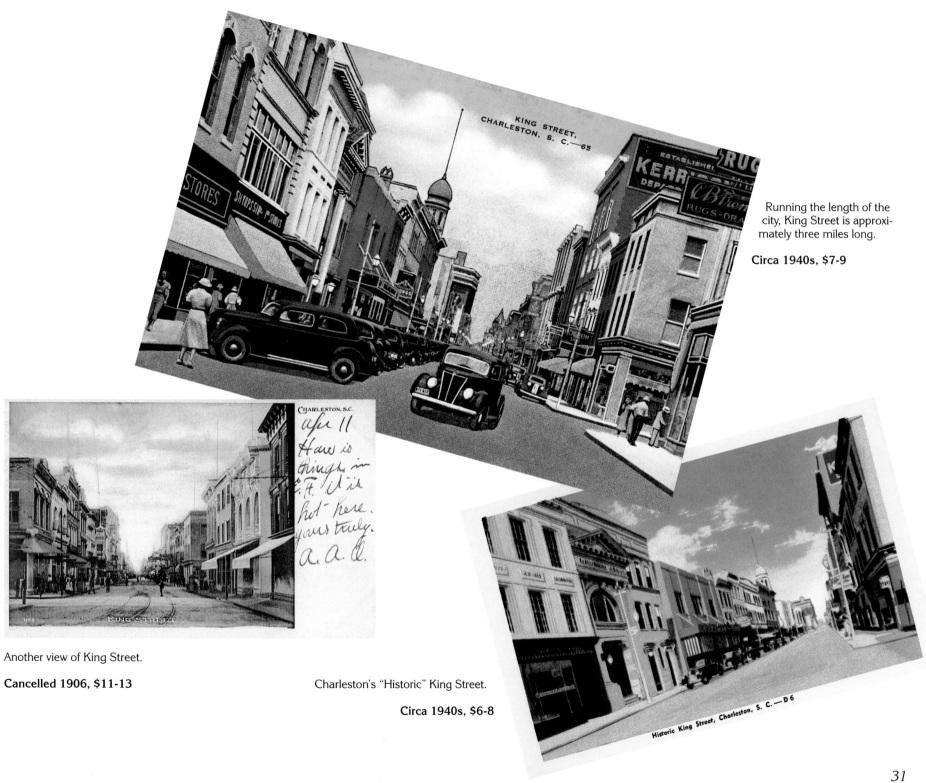

Running the length of the city, King Street is approximately three miles long.

Circa 1940s, $7-9

Another view of King Street.

Cancelled 1906, $11-13

Charleston's "Historic" King Street.

Circa 1940s, $6-8

Looking further south down Church Street.

Circa 1920s, $5-7

Some of the vintage houses located on St. Michael's Alley.

Circa 1920s, $5-7

Another view of Church Street.

Circa 1920s, $6-8

Church Street showing St. Phillip's and the Huguenot Church.

Circa 1940s, $4-6

CHURCH STREET   SHOWING HUGUENOT AND ST. PHILIP'S CHURCH. CHARLESTON, S. C.

Looking down Stoll's Alley.

Circa 1920s, $5-7

A view of Church Street showing the
Old First Baptist Church.

Circa 1920s, $5-7

"There's a bit of the town / That you can't ignore, / If
you're poking around / With intent to explore." E.P.V.

Circa 1950s, $4-6

STOLL'S ALLEY SHOP

CHURCH STREET, NEAR WATER STREET   CHARLESTON, SOUTH CAROLINA

MURRAY BOULEVARD, CHARLESTON, S. C.

Named for A.B. Murray, "whose generosity made this development possible," Murray Boulevard is located along the South Battery.

Circa 1920s, $3-5

Old Beaufain Street, Charleston, S. C.

A view of Beaufain Street.

Circa 1900s, $3-5

Murray Boulevard, "one of the most beautiful drives in the entire South."

Cancelled 1907, $3-5

MURRAY BOULEVARD, CHARLESTON, S. C.—48

Live oaks draped with Spanish moss line both sides of this lovely avenue.

Circa 1920s, $2-4

Archdale Street located near King and Broad Streets.

Circa 1910s, $11-13

A 12587 Old Quaint Archdale St., Charleston, S. C.

COLONIAL LAKE & RUTTEDGE ST., CHARLESTON S.C.

Rutledge Avenue bordering Colonial Lake.

Cancelled 1907, $3-5

35

South Bay Street home to a number of magnificent houses.

Circa 1900s, $7-9

South Bay Street.
Charleston, S. C.

A view of East Broad Street showing the old Post Office in the distance.

Circa 1900s, $7-9

10554. EAST BROAD STREET, CHARLESTON, S. C.   SHOWING OLD POST OFFICE IN DISTANCE

The corner of Broad and Meeting Streets showing City Hall and St. Michael's Church.

Circa 1900s, $7-8

Like King Street, Meeting Street runs the whole length of the city.

Circa 1910s, $10-12

Another view of Meeting Street, this one showing St. Michael's and the Post Office.

Cancelled 1909, $6-8

Public Buildings and Schools

Like many of its houses and other important buildings, the public buildings in Charleston reflect the city's style as well as its history. Some, like the old Exchange Building, are as much tourist attractions as they are buildings for public use. Even the ones that are still mainly public buildings have features to appeal to city visitors. City Hall, for example, holds an excellent collection of historic relics and artwork that is open to public viewing during regular business hours. John Trumbull's portrait of George Washington has a most intriguing history and is a must for visitors. A number of Charleston's public buildings are listed on the National Register of Historic Places. Charleston is also home to a number of excellent public and private schools as well as several universities, including the College of Charleston, which is the oldest college in the state and the thirteenth oldest in the nation.

In 1767 the Exchange building was converted into an exchange and custom house where stamp taxed tea was stored.

Circa 1940s, $5-7

The Old Exchange Building, Charleston, S. C.

C. T. 10—Exchange Building, Charleston, S. C.

The Exchange Building is one of the most historic buildings in Charleston. Pirates like Stede Bonnet were confined here in 1718, and during the Revolutionary War the Provincial Congress had its meetings in this building.

Circa 1940s, $5-7

OLD POST OFFICE, CHARLESTON, S. C.

From 1818-1896, the Exchange building was the Post Office for the city of Charleston.

Circa 1930s, $4-6

Y. M. C. A., Charleston, S. C.

The Charleston Y.M.C.A. was constructed at a cost of $157,000 all raised by popular subscription.

Cancelled 1929, $8-10

Located beneath the Old Exchange Building the Provost "Dungeon" has housed such notables as pirate Stede Bonnet and Continental Army Colonel Isaac Hayne. It has also held taxed tea seized by the inhabitants of Charleston and it sheltered gun powder from the Old Powder Magazine.

Circa 1930s, $4-6

Dungeons of the "Provost." Charleston. S.C.

Charleston, S. C. City Hall - This Building contains the most valuable collection of paintings in Charleston.

In addition to its government offices, Charleston City Hall also featured a large collection of oil paintings, and a small historical museum both of which are open for public viewing.

Circa 1910s, $6-8

Y. M. C. A. BUILDING, CHARLESTON, S. C.

The Charleston Y.M.C.A. boasted a membership of 1,600 and its outdoor athletic field was "one of the finest in the United States."

Circa 1900s, $6-8

CITY HALL, CHARLESTON, S. C.—81

City Hall is noted for its collection of priceless historic artifacts and artwork including the famous painting of George Washington by artist John Trumbull.

Circa 1940s, $5-7

POST OFFICE, CHARLESTON, S. C.   74783

The Charleston Post Office was built in 1896 and replaced the one located in the Exchange Building.

Circa 1920s, $5-7

Post Office, Charleston, S. C.

Another view of the Post Office from the corner of Meeting and Broad Streets.

Cancelled 1913, $6-8

10180. POST OFFICE, CHARLESTON, S. C.

The Post Office is located on the corner of Broad and Meeting Streets opposite St. Michael's Church.

Circa 1900s, $6-8

CHARLESTON, S.C.—OLD COUNTY COURT HOUSE TO LEFT AND CITY HALL

A view of City Hall and the Old County Courthouse.

Cancelled 1908, $7-9

Built in the Spanish Renaissance style, the New Union Station marked a period of rapid commercial progress in Charleston.

Circa 1910s, $10-12

An aerial view of Roper Hospital.

Circa 1940s, $4-6

City Hall was was originally built in 1801 for the Charleston branch of the First Bank of the United States Bank.

Circa 1900s, $6-8

The old Roper Hospital operated in Charleston from 1850 until the building was destroyed in 1905.

Cancelled 1905, $5-7

Founded in 1773, the Charleston Chamber of Commerce is the oldest chamber of commerce in the United States.

Circa 1940s, $4-6

On January 1, 1931 the Charleston Free Library opened in the Charleston Museum Building. It moved to a new location on the corner of Montague Street and Rutledge Avenue in 1935 and still later to Marion Square.

Cancelled 1937, $3-5

Currently the Custom Building houses the Weather Bureau as well as the Customs Department.

Circa 1930s, $4-6

Located on the Cooper River, the Custom House was built in 1850.

Circa 1900s, $5-7

Memminger High School, one of Charleston's several public schools.

Cancelled 1913, $5-7

The Mitchell School, Charleston, S. C.

Craft School
Charleston, S. C.

The Craft School.

Circa 1900s, $5-7

Mitchell Elementary School, located on Perry Street.

Circa 1910s, $4-6

COLLEGE OF CHARLESTON
ONE OF THE OLDEST COLLEGES IN U. S. A.
CHARLESTON, S. C.—92

Chartered in 1785, the College of Charleston
was the first city college in the United States.

Circa 1940s, $4-6

Wm. Enston Home Entrance
Charleston, S. C.

The entrance to the William Enston Home. The construction of the home began in 1886 and many of the cottages on the grounds were completed in 1889.

Circa 1900s, $4-6

Baker-Craig Sanatorium, Charleston, S. C.

Established on the shores of Colonial Lake, Baker-Craig Sanitarium provided a restful haven away from the busyness of the rest of the city.

Circa 1900s, $5-7

Charleston, S. C. The William Enston Home to make old age comfortable.

William Enston, the Home's benefactor, bequeathed most of his estate to establish a home for the city's elderly and infirm that would "make old age comfortable."

Circa 1910s, $4-6

Charleston, S. C. Orphan Home - one of the oldest in the U.S. - Built by Soldiers of the Revolution

The Charleston Orphan Home was built by veterans of the Revolutionary War and was one of the oldest in the United States.

Circa 1900s, $4-6

Important Buildings

Charleston is home to a number of buildings that are worth noting for their cultural, historical, and architectural significance. The city has one of the most complete historical districts in the country with more than 1400 historically significant buildings. A number of these buildings date back to the days when Charleston was one of the shining stars of the South when it was filled to overflowing with money from the trade of rice, indigo and cotton. Others go back even further to the Revolutionary War when the city and the rest of the colonies struggled to free themselves from the overbearing rule of Great Britain. A few go back further still to the days when Charleston was Charles Town and the colony was struggling to make its way in a new and foreign land. Some, like the Market House, are held up as Charleston's finest examples of different architectural style. Others are noted for their cultural significance, offering glimpses into the style and behavior of Charlestonians past and present.

The Old Powder Magazine on Cumberland Street was built in the early days of the colony to store "powder, armes, and other stores, and habiliments of war."

Circa 1900s, $4-6

During the Revolutionary War, the Magazine was put to use again, storing arms and powder for the Continental Army.

Circa 1940s, $3-5

Old Powder Magazine, Charleston, S. C.

Old Powder Magazine, Charleston, S. C.

In 1901, the South Carolina Society of Colonial Dames purchased the Old Powder Magazine. It was restored and converted into a chapter room and museum.

Circa 1910s, $3-5

After the Revolutionary War, the Powder Magazine was privately owned and maintained until the 1886 earthquake.

Circa 1910s, $3-5

Formerly known as the "Rodgers Mansion," the Scottish Rite Cathedral has been called "a unique specimen of architecture." Visitors to the Cathedral were welcome at all times.

Circa 1910s, $4-6

SCOTTISH RITE CATHEDRAL, CHARLESTON, S. C.

88701

According to legend, the Pirate House on Church Street was the headquarters for a number of local pirate bands that sailed in the waters around Charleston and the Atlantic Ocean.

Circa 1920s, $4-6

In 1878 the Old Slave Market was remodeled into a tenement dwelling. In 1938 it was purchased by Miriam B. Wilson and converted into a museum of African-American culture, history, and art.

Circa 1920s, $3-5

A 1856 city ordinance forbidding the public sale of slaves led to the establishment of private auction halls like this one built by Thomas Ryan, a city alderman.

Circa 1920s, $3-5

49

The Pirate House Charleston, S. C.

Due to the efforts of Governor Robert Johnson and Colonel William Rhett, Charleston and the surrounding areas were made safe and a significant number of pirates were either captured or killed.

Circa 1920s, $5-7

Phillip's Church from Courtyard of The Pirate House Charleston, S. C.

The spire of St. Phillip's Church was clearly visible from the courtyard of the Pirate House.

Circa 1930s, $3-5

PINK HOUSE, PRE-REVOLUTIONARY TAVERN, CHARLESTON, S. C.

Located on Chalmers Street, the Pink House stands opposite the Old Slave Market.

Circa 1940s, $2-4

No longer a buccaneer hangout, the Pirate House is now viewed by tourists interested in the fascinating early history of Charleston.

Circa 1940s, $2-4

PIRATE HOUSE GARDEN, CHARLESTON, S. C.

Named for its unique color, the Pink House is three stories high with only one room on each floor.

Circa 1940s, $3-5

One of the oldest buildings in Charleston, the Pink House was a tavern built in 1712 by John Breton.

Circa 1930s, $3-5

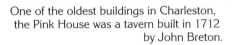

The first City Market was established some time between 1788 and 1804. The current building, Market Hall, was built in 1841.

Circa 1940s, $3-5

THE OLD MARKET, CHARLESTON, S. C.—37

While the sheds behind the building are still used as a public market, the main building of the Old Market Building now houses the Confederate Museum.

Circa 1940s, $3-5

THE OLD MARKET, CHARLESTON, S. C.

While it was by no means the first market built in Charleston, the Old Market Building is currently the only surviving market building in the city.

Cancelled 1917, $4-6

11533 CENTRAL MARKET AND THE BUZZARDS, CHARLESTON, S. C.   A PART OF THE OLD SLAVE MARKET

Since market vendors were allowed to sell only fresh wares, anything remaining at the end of the day was usually thrown out. Buzzards would eat the garbage and helped to keep the area around the market clean.

Circa 1900s, $4-6

The Huguenot Tavern
Church and Queen Sts.,
Charleston, S.C.

Where can be had
distinctive dishes
and desserts of
old Charles Town

"Jolly Corner"

"A merrie place in days of yore"

"The Provost," & Old French Tavern, East Bay St. Charleston, S.C.

This small tavern on East Bay Street is located across from the Old Exchange building. The building is marked "French Coffee House, formerly 'Harris Tavern.'"

Circa 1930s, $3-5

Located on the northwest corner of Church and Queen Streets, the Huguenot Tavern once served as a waiting room for passengers traveling by stagecoach between Charleston, Augusta, Savannah, and all points west.

Circa 1920s, $4-6

People's Office Building, Broad St.,
Charleston, S. C.

Built in 1826, this building in Washington Square is the headquarters of the South Carolina Historical Society. It has long been claimed to be the first fireproof building constructed in America.

Circa 1930s, $5-7

Located on Broad Street, the People's Office Building housed a number of public and small business offices.

Circa 1920s, $4-6

Houses

Charleston is known for its distinctive single house style. The typical Charleston house is the classic Georgian house with its gable turned to the street and with piazzas on the side. Charleston houses proved to be very popular with visitors, so popular in fact, that before the formation of organizations like the Preservation Society of Charleston and Historic Charleston Foundation, pieces and sometimes whole houses were taken home as souvenirs. Today a number of Charleston's historic houses operate as public museums, giving visitors a glimpse of the lives, manners, and styles of past residents.

Old Residences on Legare Street, Charleston, S.C.

206,661. J.Y.

Historic residences on Legare Street.

Circa 1900s, $5-7

Another old colonial Charleston single house.

Circa 1900s, $4-6

The McCardy House, one of many well-to-do homes located on South Battery.

Circa 1920s, $4-6

Built by John Fraser, a wealthy shipping magnate and blockade runner, this home on East Battery is located on land granted by the Lords Proprietors in 1681.

Cancelled 1961, $6-8

The Old Holmes House, East Battery, Charleston, S.C.

This house was the home of Emma Holmes, the Charleston native who chronicled events of the Civil War in her diary of 1861-1866. The work has gained historical significance because of the in-depth descriptions of events as they happened in Charleston.

Cancelled 1909, $6-8

Rice planter Daniel Heyward built the Heyward-Washington House in 1772 as a town house for his son, Thomas Heyward Jr. The house gained additional fame when George Washington stayed there during his week-long visit in May of 1791.

Circa 1930s, $5-7

HEYWARD-WASHINGTON HOUSE AND CABBAGE ROW   CHARLESTON, S. C.
DRAWN BY ELIZABETH O'NEILL VERNER
S ATLANTIC STREET

The interior of the Heyward-Washington House. The house was bought in 1929 by the Charleston Museum and was the first historic house museum in Charleston.

Circa 1930s, $3-5

The residence of Miss Sallie Calhoun Carrington, located on the corner of Meeting Street and the Battery.

Cancelled 1944, $5-7

Residence of Miss Sallie Calhoun Carrington   Corner Meeting Street and the Battery   Charleston, S. C.

DRAWING ROOM OF MILES BREWTON (PRINGLE) RESIDENCE, CHARLESTON   F-3   PHOTO BY BAYARD WOOTTEN

The Drawing Room of the Pringle House. The house was open to visitors for the admission fee of one dollar. Tea was served in the dining room from 3 P.M. to 5 P.M. for no additional charge. It is now a private residence.

Circa 1920s, $5-7

PRINGLE HOUSE, CHARLESTON, S. C.

Built by Colonel Miles Brewton in 1765, the Brewton (or as many Charlestonians say, the Pringle) House remained in the same family for five generations.

Circa 1940s, $4-6

The Pringle House has had a long and distinguished history, serving as the headquarters for British Troops in 1780 and Federal troops at the end of the Civil War.

Circa 1920s, $4-6

In addition to its historical value the Pringle House is also well-known for the style of its architecture.

Circa 1940s, $4-6

Another of the many beautiful historic homes found throughout Charleston.

Circa 1940s, $3-5

Located on East Bay Street, this row of houses has been nicknamed "Rainbow Row" because of the bright and varied colors.

Cancelled 1955, $3-5

Bright colored azaleas light up the lawn in front of Yeamans Hall.

Circa 1930s, $3-5

In the summer of 1671, Sir John Yeamans settled in the area around Charleston with around fifty settlers from the British colony of Barbados.

Circa 1930s, $4-6

Guest cottages located on the grounds of Yeamans Hall.

Cancelled 1938, $4-6

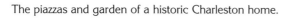
70251 GALLERY AND GARDEN, CHARLESTON, S. C.   COPR. DETROIT PUBLISHING CO.

The piazzas and garden of a historic Charleston home.

Circa 1930s, $4-6

The Pettigrew House on St. Michael's Alley.

Circa 1920s, $6-8

Number 18 Meeting Street.

Circa 1930s, $5-7

Hutty House and Studio, Tradd Street, Charleston, South Carolina

The Alfred Hutty House and Studio on Tradd near King Street.

Circa 1930s, $4-6

The Maybank House, also located on Meeting Street.

Circa 1930s, $4-6

63

ASHLEY HALL, CHARLESTON, S. C.

Ashley Hall, Charleston, S. C.

Once owned by the Trenholm family, Ashley Hall is currently the home of a private day school for girls. First Lady Barbara Bush was once a boarding student here.

Circa 1930s, $3-5

Built in 1815, Ashley Hall is one of the most stately old homes in Charleston.

Circa 1940s, $3-5

Gates

An interesting aspect of Charleston's style can be found in the wrought iron gates that mark the entrances to many of the city's houses and older buildings. Some, like the Sword Gates on Legare Street, were made in England and shipped to Charleston. Most of the gates of the eighteenth and nineteenth centuries were made by local craftsmen.

Located on Legare Street, the Smyth Gateway is one of Charleston's many beautiful wrought iron gates.

Circa 1930s, $4-6

The Marshall Gate on Church Street.

Circa 1930s, $4-6

Charleston is noted for its many wrought iron gateways and grills, like the Smyth Gateway on Legare Street.

Circa 1940s, $2-4

A simple wrought iron gate and fence at 28 Chapel Street.

Circa 1940s, $3-5

Another view of the Smyth Gateway on Legare Street.

Circa 1910s, $4-6

Fashioned mostly in the 18th and 19th centuries, almost all of the iron gates in Charleston were the work of local craftsman.

Circa 1940s, $2-4

The spire of St. Michael's Church as seen through a gateway on Tradd Street.

Circa 1930s, $4-6

The Simonton Gateway, Charleston, S. C.—29

The Sword Gates Gateway of Simonton House,
Charleston, S. C.

Brought to Charleston from England, the Sword Gates are considered one of the finest examples of early wrought iron work.

Circa 1940s, $2-4

The gateway to the Simonton House is called the Sword Gate because of the sword motif found in the scroll work.

Circa 1920s, $2-4

The Simonton House on Legare Street was built in 1776, the gates and gateway were placed there sometime between 1815-1820.

Circa 1940s, $2-4

GATEWAY OF SIMONTON HOUSE, BUILT 1776, CHARLESTON, S. C.

2A-H530

The gates in front of St. Phillip's Church are said to be possessed of "an especial dignity and beauty."

Circa 1940s, $2-4

Gateway to St. Philip's Church, Charleston, S.C.

Made by hand, the gates of St. Phillip's are fine examples of colonial craftsmanship.

Cancelled 1947, $2-4

LESESNE GATES   CHARLESTON, S. C.

DRAWN BY ELIZABETH O'NEILL VERNER
38 TRADD STREET

The Lesesne Gates in front of the Citadel the Military College of South Carolina.

Circa 1930s, $3-5

Churches

As with a number of British colonies, Carolina was home to a diverse and eclectic population, particularly when it came to religion. The Lords Proprietors, in the hopes of attracting a large number of settlers in a short amount of time, advertised religious tolerance and freedom of worship for those who would settle in their colony. The advertisements worked wonders, attracting religious minorities from not only England but from other countries in Europe as well. Huguenots from France, Presbyterians from Scotland, Sephardic Jews from Spain and Portugal, as well as Quakers and Anglicans from England came to Charleston, attracted by the offers of free land and freedom from religious persecution. The diversity in religion had several side effects, one of them being the large number of churches built in the city; so many that Charleston was given the nickname, "The Holy City."

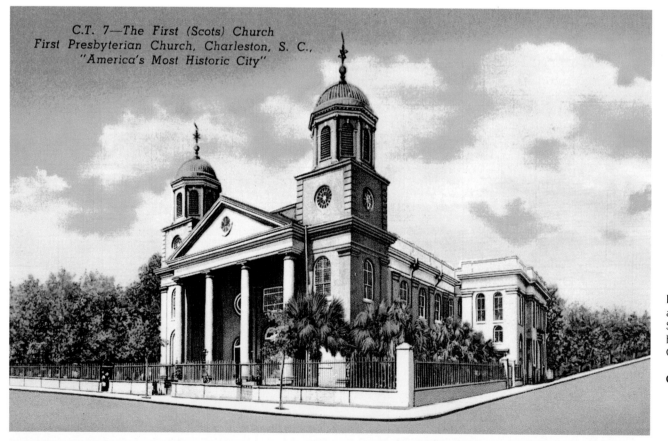

C.T. 7—The First (Scots) Church
First Presbyterian Church, Charleston, S. C.,
"America's Most Historic City"

Located on the corner of Meeting and Tradd Streets, the First Scots Presbyterian Church was built in 1814 by James and John Gordon.

Circa 1940s, $3-5

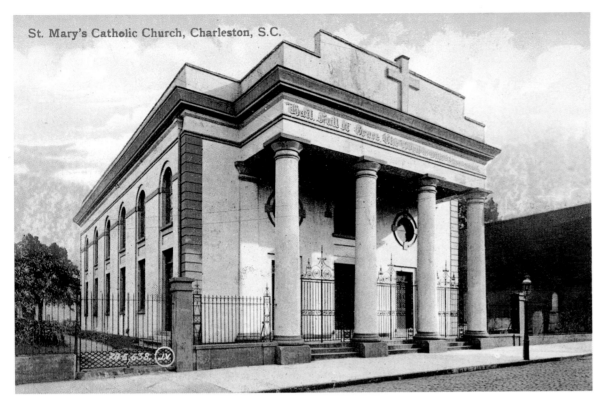

St. Mary's Catholic Church, Charleston, S.C.

St. Mary's Roman Catholic Church on Hasell Street is the first Roman Catholic Church in the Carolinas and Georgia. The present building was built in 1839.

Circa 1900s, $4-6

Before the completion of the building of St. John's Lutheran Church in 1818, the congregation worshipped in the French Huguenot Church.

Cancelled 1941, $4-6

Interior of St. John's Lutheran Church, Charleston, S. C.

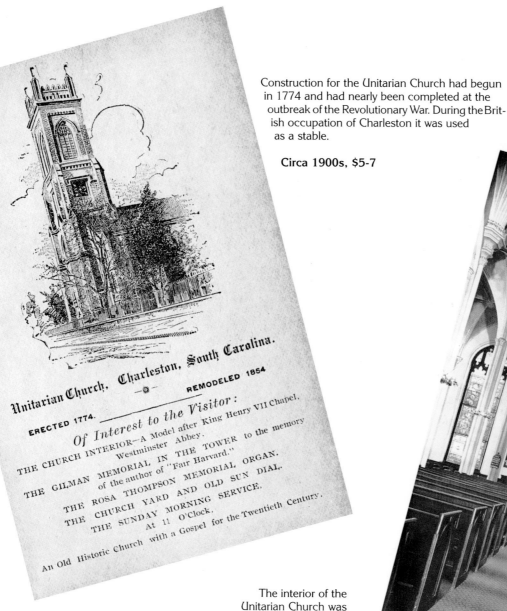

Unitarian Church, Charleston, South Carolina.

ERECTED 1774. REMODELED 1854

Of Interest to the Visitor:

THE CHURCH INTERIOR—A Model after King Henry VII Chapel, Westminster Abbey.

THE GILMAN MEMORIAL IN THE TOWER to the memory of the author of "Fair Harvard."

THE ROSA THOMPSON MEMORIAL ORGAN.

THE CHURCH YARD AND OLD SUN DIAL.

THE SUNDAY MORNING SERVICE, At 11 O'Clock,

An Old Historic Church with a Gospel for the Twentieth Century.

Construction for the Unitarian Church had begun in 1774 and had nearly been completed at the outbreak of the Revolutionary War. During the British occupation of Charleston it was used as a stable.

Circa 1900s, $5-7

The Unitarian Church, 4 Archdale St., Charleston, S. C.

The interior of the Unitarian Church was modeled after the Chapel of Henry VII in Westminster Abby.

Circa 1920s, $4-6

Constructed out of Connecticut brownstone, the Cathedral of St. John-the-Baptist is widely regarded as "one of the most magnificent buildings in the south."

Circa 1940s, $4-6

The Cathedral of St. John-the-Baptist is approximately 200 feet long with a sixty foot ceiling. The windows were imported from Munich.

Cancelled 1908, $4-6

73

A number of Charleston's early settlers were Huguenots (French Protestants). Upon arriving, they established a church near St. Phillip's on Church Street.

Circa 1930s, $5-7

Originally called St. Finbar's Cathedral, the cathedral was rededicated the Cathedral of St. John-the-Baptist in 1906 after a fire destroyed the old building.

Circa 1900s, $5-7

Completed in 1845, the current French Huguenot Church is the third church building to occupy this location.

Circa 1930s, $5-7

French Huguenot Church, Charleston, South Carolina

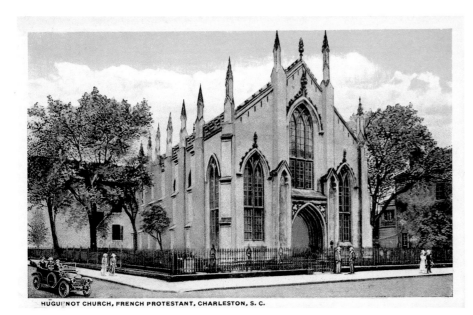

Currently, the congregation of the French Huguenot Church is the only French Calvinist congregation in the United States.

Circa 1920s, $5-7

The original building of St. Andrew's Parish Church was built in 1706. Additions were added on in 1723 to make the building into the shape of a cross.

Circa 1930s, $4-6

Nicknamed "The Holy City," Charleston is home to a number of historic churches like the Citadel Square Baptist Church established in 1856.

Circa 1940s, $4-6

The oldest church building in Charleston, the cornerstone of St. Michael's Episcopal Church was laid in 1752 and opened for worship in 1761.

Circa 1930s, $3-5

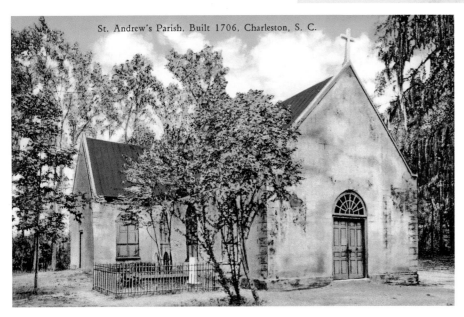

In 1764, St. Andrew's Parish Church was partially destroyed in a fire. It was rebuilt in its present shape later that same year.

Circa 1940s, $3-5

St. Michael's bells and clock were brought to Charleston from England in 1764 and its organ four years later.

Circa 1940s, $4-6

ST. MICHAEL'S CHURCH, CHARLESTON, S. C.

65987-N

Founded in 1750 and built in 1840, Kahal Kadosh Beth Elohim is the oldest reform synagogue in the United States.

Circa 1940s, $4-6

During his 1791 visit to Charleston, President George Washington attended St. Michael's afternoon worship service.

Circa 1920s, $5-7

The interior of Goose Creek Church. According the legend, the Church was not destroyed by British soldiers because of the British Coat-of-Arms displayed inside.

Circa 1930s, $3-5

The Goose Creek Church was established in 1713 and is one of the oldest churches in the state.

Circa 1930s, $3-5

St. Phillip's Church is one of Charleston's oldest churches. It was built in 1723 and restored after a fire in 1835. Because of its age and historic significance, St. Phillip's has been called "the Mother Church of Charleston."

Circa 1940s, $4-6

Old Goose Creek Church (Episcopal). Built 1713 near Charleston, S. C.

Patches of Spanish moss drape their tendrils around the outside of the Goose Creek Church.

Circa 1910s, $3-5

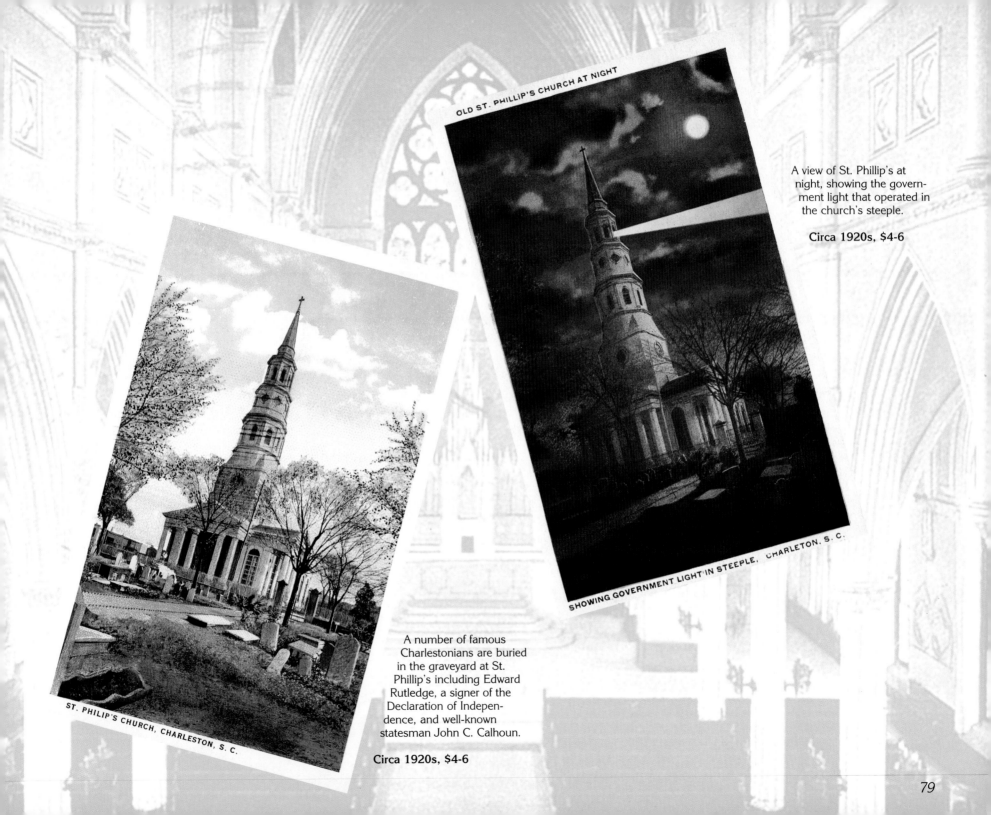

OLD ST. PHILLIP'S CHURCH AT NIGHT

A view of St. Phillip's at night, showing the government light that operated in the church's steeple.

Circa 1920s, $4-6

SHOWING GOVERNMENT LIGHT IN STEEPLE, CHARLETON, S. C.

ST. PHILIP'S CHURCH, CHARLESTON, S. C.

A number of famous Charlestonians are buried in the graveyard at St. Phillip's including Edward Rutledge, a signer of the Declaration of Independence, and well-known statesman John C. Calhoun.

Circa 1920s, $4-6

The Citadel and Porter Military Academy

The Citadel was originally established as a place to train municipal guards. The Governor of South Carolina at that time, John P. Richardson, decided that the military training should be supplemented with some system of education. In 1842, the South Carolina Legislature established the South Carolina Military Academy.

The Citadel soon became known for the quality of its education and the quality of military discipline displayed by students and graduates. During the Civil War, Citadel graduates as well as cadets served in the Confederate Army, mounting and operating heavy cannons, escorting prisoners, and serving on guard duty. After the Civil War, the Citadel was closed and did not reopen until 1882. The Citadel was originally located on Marion Square and was moved to its present location on the Ashley River in 1922.

The Porter Military Academy was founded as the Holy Communion Church Institute by the Reverend A. Toomer Porter, an Episcopal priest, in 1879, to educate former soldiers and children left destitute or orphaned after the Civil War. The Academy was located on the site of a former Federal arsenal on Ashley Street. In the nineteenth century, the Institute changed its name to the Porter Military Academy. The grounds and the buildings were purchased by the Medical University of South Carolina in 1964.

The Citadel, Charleston, S. C.

T22

Founded in 1842, the Citadel was first established as a school of arts as well as arms.

Circa 1940s, $4-6

Administration Building of The Citadel, Military College, Charleston, S. C. — D 8

Bond Hall, the Citadel's main academic and administrative building.

Cancelled 1944, $4-6

Charleston, S. C. South Carolina Military Academy showing Fountain and Old Stone Relic

Visitors stroll around Marion Square in front of the Old Citadel pausing to admire a fountain or the remains of Charleston's old defenses.

Circa 1900s, $3-5

South Carolina Military Academy, Charleston, S. C.
Second to West Point.

South Carolina's premier military academy, the Citadel.

Cancelled 1916, $4-6

Dress Parade, The Citadel, Charleston, S. C.

Citadel cadets stand at attention during a dress parade.

Circa 1940s, $3-5

C. T. 15—Full-Dress Parade, the Citadel, Charleston, S. C.

The Citadel is a state-operated four year college. It offers courses in ten elective fields as well as R.O.T.C. units.

Cancelled 1941, $4-6

*1606 — South Carolina
Military Academy,
Charleston, S. C.*

Cadets in full-dress pose in Marion
Square in front of the Old Citadel.

Circa 1900s, $5-7

The Armory at the
Citadel.

Cancelled 1942, $5-7

The Armory, The Citadel, Charleston, South Carolina

A view of the Old Citadel showing the Calhoun Monument and Marion Square.

Circa 1900s, $5-7

The nonsectarian Cadet Chapel at the Citadel does not belong to any particular denomination.

Circa 1940s, $4-6

Views of Bond Hall, the Cadet Chapel, and the front gates of the Citadel.

Circa 1940s, $5-7

The Citadel, Charleston, S. C.

On January 9, 1861 Cadets from the Citadel fired artillery from Morris Island at the *Star of the West*, a Union supply ship. The cadets were chosen by the city because they were the best qualified to operate the artillery.

Circa 1900s, $5-7

Originally called the Holy Communion Church Institute, the Porter Military Academy was founded to educate former soldiers and children left orphaned or destitute by the Civil War.

Cancelled 1910, $3-5

Charleston, S. C. Porter Military Academy.

Founded by Reverend A. Toomer Porter, the Porter Military Academy was located on Ashley Avenue, occupying the site of a former Federal arsenal.

Cancelled 1902, $4-6

CHARLESTON, S. C.— PORTER MILITARY ACADEMY.

Water

Water has played an important part in Charleston's development socially as well as economically. Located on a peninsula between the Ashley and Cooper Rivers, the city is surrounded by water. Ships came to Charleston bringing rum, slaves, and luxury items from England and the Caribbean and taking rice, indigo, cotton, and hides to England and other colonies. Water has played an important role in the city's historical development as well. During the Revolutionary War, Charleston's strategic location as a port was well understood by the British, who attacked the city twice during the course of the war. Later in the Civil War, Charleston's value as a port city was reaffirmed by the efforts of the Union Navy to blockade the city. The efforts were only partially successful and Charleston soon became a frequent port of call for blockade runners.

After the Civil War, Charleston's naval fortunes improved when the United States Navy built a dry dock in Charleston in 1909. One of the most important naval establishments south of Norfolk, the Charleston Navy Yard remained active through World War II, the Korean, and Vietnam Wars.

Charleston's waterways were also ideal for pleasure boating and the waters of Charleston Harbor and the Cooper and Ashley Rivers were often covered with all manner of private sailing and fishing boats.

Championship snipe racing in Charleston Harbor. The harbor is an excellent place for boating and Charleston has hosted a number of international water sporting events.

Circa 1940s, $3-5

Instead of building a new structure to serve as the administration building for the U.S. Navy Yard at Charleston, an existing one, the Trumbull Home, was remodeled to fit the Yard's needs.

Circa 1910s, $5-7

The Officer's Quarters of the Marine Barracks at the Navy Yard.

Circa 1920s, $4-6

The Navy Yard's Commanding Officer's Quarters. The Navy Yard was located on Meeting Street. It was the most important naval establishment south of Norfolk and cost roughly $5,000,000.

Cancelled 1912, $4-6

A dry-dock at the Navy Yard stands empty awaiting its next project.

Circa 1910, $6-8

Crowds gather at the Navy Yard to watch the launching of a newly completed destroyer.

Cancelled 1941, $4-6

The Ashley River Bridge cost $1,200,000 to build and was dedicated on May 6, 1926 to the South Carolina soldiers who died in World War I.

Circa 1940s, $4-6

The Ashley River Memorial Bridge is an important link between Florida and the north Atlantic states.

Circa 1940s, $3-5

ASHLEY RIVER BRIDGE, CHARLESTON, S. C.—58

The Ashley River Bridge has been declared by prominent engineering authorities to be "one of the most beautiful structures in the United States."

Circa 1940s, $2-4

The John P. Grace Memorial Bridge also known as The Cooper River Bridge Charleston, S. C.

Also known as the Cooper River Bridge, the John P. Grace Memorial Bridge was 295 feet tall at its highest point and the lights on the bridge could be seen from fifty miles away.

Circa 1940s, $2-4

COOPER RIVER BRIDGE, CHARLESTON, S. C.—63

The Cooper River Bridge was roughly three miles long, was made from 14,500 feet of steelwork, and spanned two bodies of water, the Cooper River and Town Creek.

Circa 1938, $2-4

Costing roughly $6,000,000, the Cooper River Bridge was "unlike any other bridge in the world as to size, length, height, and design." Now demolished, it has been replaced by a higher and more modern bridge.

Cancelled 1950, $3-5

COOPER RIVER BRIDGE, CHARLESTON, S. C.—71

Colonial Lake, Charleston, S. C.

Colonial Lake, situated along Rutledge Avenue, Beaufain, and Broad Street.

Cancelled 1910, $5-7

VIEWS OF BEAUTIFUL COLONIAL LAKE, CHARLESTON, S. C.

Views of Colonial Lake and some of the houses bordering it.

Circa 1920s, $5-7

C. T. 2—Beautiful Colonial Lake showing the Baker Sanitorium in Background, Charleston, S. C.

A view of the park and gardens around Colonial Lake and of Baker Sanitorium across the lake. Colonial Lake is a salt water lake and the level of the water is controlled by tide gates.

Circa 1940s, $3-5

COLONIAL LAKE, CHARLESTON, S. C.

U. S. ARMY HOSPITAL SHIP "SHAMROCK" ARRIVES AT PORT OF EMBARKATION CHARLESTON, S. C.

Photo by U. S. Army Signal Corps

During the summer, a number of aquatic sports are held on Colonial Lake.

Cancelled 1902, $3-5

The Army hospital ship *Shamrock* arriving in Charleston Harbor.

Circa 1930s, $11-13

CHARLESTON, S.C. COLONIAL LAKE.

Charleston was called the "Venice of America" because of the creeks and ponds found throughout the city limits. Colonial Lake is one of the few ponds that remain.

Circa 1910s, $4-6

CHARLESTON, S.C.

A clipper ship and two smaller vessels sailing the waters of Charleston Harbor.

Circa 1910s, $4-6

NEW CLYDE LINE DOCKS, CHARLESTON, S. C.

The new Clyde Line Docks along the Charleston Waterfront.

Circa 1920s, $6-8

Charleston's Mosquito Fleet, a fleet of small row and motor boats that ply the back waterways of Charleston Harbor and the Ashley and Cooper Rivers.

Circa 1930s, $7-9

THE MOSQUITO FLEET, CHARLESTON, SOUTH CAROLINA

WATERFRONT VIEW OF CHARLESTON, S. C. FROM COOPER RIVER   —*Photo by Bayard Wootten*

A view of the Charleston Waterfront from the Cooper River. The Custom House and the spire of St. Phillip's Church are clearly visible.

Circa 1930s, $7-9

VIEW OF FORT SUMTER AND HARBOR FROM BATTERY, CHARLESTON, S. C.   —*Photo by Bayard Wooten*

A view of the Harbor and Fort Sumter from the Battery.

Circa 1930s, $3-5

WATERFRONT   CHARLESTON, S. C.

©DRAWN BY ELIZABETH O'NEILL VERNER
38 TRADD STREET

Sailboats bob on the waves just off the edge of the Charleston Waterfront.

Circa 1930s, $5-7

Harbor of Charleston, S. C. and Birds-Eye view of City.

A birds-eye view of Charleston and the harbor beyond.

Circa 1900s, $6-8

1610—*Charleston Harbor, Charleston S. C.*

When Charleston was first founded its chief exports were rice, indigo, and deer hides. Today it is still a busy port city, which sees a large amount of shipping traffic.

Circa 1900s, $6-8

Hotels

As long as guests have been coming to Charleston, there have been hotels waiting to give them a place to rest and enjoy their stay. One of the first hotels in the city was the Planter's Hotel built on the site of the old Queen Street Theater. The hotel was erected in 1809 and was used by planters who would come to Charleston for the horse racing season. The hotel was very popular and well known for the quality of its food and drink. A number of hotels like the Fort Sumter and Francis Marion Hotels were built during the 1920s. Charleston was also home to several smaller guest houses for those wishing a quieter, more home-like stay in the Palmetto City.

Home of Mrs. John Fergusson Girardeau
182 Tradd St., Corner of Ashley Ave., Charleston, 21, South Carolina — Dial 8720

The home of Mrs. John Fergusson Giradeau on the corner of Tradd Street and Ashley Avenue overlooking the Ashley River.

Circa 1930s, $7-9

1608—Charleston Hotel, Charleston, S. C.

Now demolished, the Charleston Hotel was "one of the most attractive hotels in the South, noted for its imposing structure, excellent management and unexcelled cuisine."

Cancelled 1908, $7-9

Hansom cabs wait outside the Charleston Hotel to take tourists back to the train station, the harbor, or on a tour of the city.

Circa 1900s, $6-8

Located on the Battery, the Fort Sumter Hotel was named for the historic fort visible from its waterfront windows. The building has since be converted into very desirable condominiums

Circa 1940s, $4-6

Because of its excellent attributes, the Charleston Hotel was the destination for many of Charleston's winter tourists.

Cancelled 1942, $6-8

FORT SUMTER HOTEL, CHARLESTON, S. C.—18

Besides Fort Sumter, forts Johnson and Moultrie were also visible from the Fort Sumter Hotel.

Cancelled 1939, $3-5

World Sign Post,
FORT SUMTER HOTEL,
Charleston, S. C.

FORT SUMTER HOTEL
A COLONIAL HOTEL

OCEAN HIGHWAY ASSOCIATION
OFFICIALLY APPROVED MEMBER

MILES FROM / MILES FROM

PHOENIX 2237 MILES
NEW YORK 761 MILES
BERMUDA 924 MILES
MIAMI 625 MILES
HONOLULU 5214 MILES
LONDON 4640 MILES
QUEBEC 1293
KEY WEST 771 MILES
HOLLYWOOD 2675 MILES
PARIS 4383 MILES
NORTH POLE 3954 MILES
SOUTH POLE 8480 MILES

FORT SUMTER HOTEL

The World Sign Post located at the southeast corner of old Fort Sumter Hotel.

Circa 1940s, $3-5

The FRANCIS MARION HOTEL
CHARLESTON
S. C.

Besides being a world class hotel, the Francis Marion Hotel was also the first concrete monument to Revolutionary War hero General Francis Marion, also known as "The Swamp Fox."

Circa 1920s, $5-7

The South Battery Guest Home located on Council Street.

Circa 1930s, $6-8

The Francis Marion Hotel was opened in 1924. As a tribute to the hotel's namesake, the interior was decorated with scenes from General Marion's life.

Cancelled 1937, $5-7

Colonial Guest Home, Folly Beach Road, Charleston, South Carolina

The Colonial Guest Home on Folly Beach Road, operated by Mrs. J. Graham Altman.

Cancelled 1940, $6-8

THE WINDERMERE
MRS. R. E. REMINGTON, HOSTESS
A HOME OF QUIET REFINEMENT WITH ACCOMMODATIONS TO FIT YOUR NEEDS.
HALF MILE WEST OF ASHLEY RIVER BRIDGE ON U. S. HIGHWAY NO. 17, CHARLESTON, S. C.

The Windermere, "a home of quiet refinement with accommodations to fit your needs."

Circa 1940s, $5-7

Palm Villa, 64 Rutledge Ave., Charleston, S. C.

Situated on Rutledge Avenue and overlooking Colonial Lake, The Palm Villa advertised "accommodations that will please the most discriminating guests, at reasonable rates."

Circa 1940s, $3-5

COURTYARD VIEW, ST. JOHN HOTEL, CHARLESTON, S. C.

A courtyard view of St. John Hotel.

Circa 1940s, $3-5

ST. JOHN HOTEL
Meeting Corner Queen Street
CHARLESTON, S. C.
Convenient - Comfortable - Moderate Rates
PLEASING PERSONAL SERVICE
Dining Room - Free Parking

"Convenient to everything," the St. John Hotel also prided itself on providing "pleasing personal service."

Circa 1930s, $5-7

St. John Hotel on the corner of Meeting and Queen Street.

Cancelled 1914, $5-7

St. John's Hotel, Charleston, S. C.

101

DINING ROOM

A glimpse of the St. John Hotel and the hotel dining room inside.

Circa 1920s, $5-7

The courtyard behind the Brewton Inn.

Circa 1930s, $3-5

The Brewton Inn on Church Street, "a southern inn of quiet charm, with 'old time' hospitality."

Circa 1930s, $4-6

Facing the Battery and White Point Gardens, Villa Margherita was "one of the finest tourist resorts in the South."

Circa 1920s, $3-5

Villa Margherita was built and owned by Mrs. Daisy Breux Simonds, one of Charleston's many prominent citizens.

Cancelled 1938, $4-6

Villa Margherita was also considered by many in Charleston to be a "perfect example of Classic Architecture."

Circa 1910s, $4-6

Clubs

With its large population of business and society elite, Charleston was home to a number of private clubs and exclusive organizations. Some, like the German Friendly Society and Hibernian Society, were organized around nationality. Some, like the Winyah Indigo Society, were organized to encourage fraternization between members of a certain profession. Others, like the Masons and the Elks, were part of a larger national organization. Still others, like the Charleston Country Club, were organized purely along the lines of social and leisure pursuits. In fact, Charleston was home to the South Carolina Golf Club, said to be the first golf club in North America and the first one to be formed outside of the United Kingdom.

The Charleston Elks Club meeting house.

Circa 1900s, $4-6

The Charleston Commercial Club.

Circa 1900s, $5-7

Like many other buildings in the city, the Commercial Club featured multiple porches stacked one on top of the other.

Circa 1900s, $4-6

The mansion of the old Belvedere Plantation was renovated and made into the Charleston Country Club's clubhouse.

Cancelled 1925, $3-5

On the grounds of the Charleston Country Club was "one of the most beautiful golf links in this part of the country."

Circa 1910s, $3-5

Because of its location across the Ashley River, near the Ashley River Bridge, the Charleston Country Club Wapoo Links Clubhouse offered an excellent view of the city.

Circa 1920s, $4-6

Parks

Botany, agriculture, and other natural curiosities have fascinated and appealed to Charlestonians for both practical and leisurely purposes. Over the years, this fascination has led to the establishment of numerous private gardens, the Charleston Museum, and several parks located throughout the city. One of the largest was Hampton Park. Located on the outskirts of Charleston, the area was home to a race course, a public fair ground, and a Confederate prison before becoming a public park in the late 1800s. Besides Hampton Park, there were others like Post Office Park located closer to the center of the city.

Located near the Post Office, Post Office Park is one of the dozens of parks found throughout Charleston.

Circa 1920s, $4-6

The entrance to Hampton Park on Rutledge Avenue.

Cancelled 1916, $2-4

During the Civil War the area that would later become Hampton Park was used to house Union prisoners of war.

Cancelled 1907, $3-5

Fountains in Hampton Park.

Cancelled 1915, $3-4

The Hampton Park Bandstand, a site of frequent outdoor concerts.

Cancelled 1911, $3-5

Charleston, S. C. Sunken Gardens. Band Stand. Hampton Park.

4521.

The Sunken Gardens at Hampton Park.

Cancelled 1908, $3-5

THE LAKE FROM THE BAND STAND, CHARLESTON, S.C.

The lake and sunken gardens as seen from the Hampton Park Bandstand.

Circa 1910s, $2-4

COPR. DETROIT PUBLISHING CO.

70255 THE LAKE, HAMPTON PARK, CHARLESTON, S. C.

Like many other parks throughout the United States, Hampton Park was home to a small population of ducks.

Circa 1900s, $3-5

The Sunken Gardens, Hampton Park, Charleston S.C.

Park visitors pose at one of the bridges leading to the sunken gardens.

Cancelled 1909, $3-5

Bridge and Fountain in Hampton Park, Charleston, S. C.

Another view of Hampton Park featuring a fountain and a bridge. Willow trees hide the opposite end of the bridge from view.

Circa 1940s, $2-4

Public Gardens

Gardens were highly valued by the citizens of Charleston. Despite the limitations of space around their town houses, gardeners made the most of the room they had with beautiful and fragrant flowers and plants. Outside the city, wealthy planters took advantage of the available space by designing larger and more elaborate gardens for the enjoyment of family and friends.

After the Civil War, these same planters were unable to maintain their homes and gardens as they had before the war and as a result many fell into disuse and were neglected as plantations were sold or abandoned. A few, like Magnolia Plantation and Middleton Place, were opened to the community as public gardens. These proved to be popular with members of the local communities and with tourists, who came to appreciate the history of the gardens as well as the beauty and variety of the plants growing there.

Each spring thousands of tourists come to Magnolia Plantation to see the "most beautiful gardens of the world."

Circa 1940s, $2-4

Magnolia Gardens is renowned as a beauty spot for its many flowering bulbs, azaleas, camellias, wisteria-covered trees and peaceful lagoons.

Circa 1940s, $2-4

THE BROAD WALK UNDER THE OAKS, MAGNOLIA GARDENS, CHARLESTON, S. C.

2A-H535

Stately moss-covered oaks shade the Broad Walk at Magnolia Gardens.

Cancelled 1939, $2-4

According to local legend, the Reverend John Grimke Drayton built Magnolia Gardens in order to entice his future bride to come to Charleston from her native Philadelphia.

Circa 1920s, $2-4

Magnolia Gardens, Charleston, S.C.

THE LAKE, MAGNOLIA ON THE ASHLEY, CHARLESTON, S. C.

The Lake at Magnolia Gardens.

Circa 1920s, $1-3

Azaleas bloom between the gaps in a grove of cypress trees.

Circa 1930s, $1-3

CHARLESTON, S. C, Across the Lake. - Magnolia Gardens.

Looking across the lake at Magnolia Gardens.

Circa 1910s, $2-4

Each spring, blooming azaleas are Magnolia Gardens' main attraction.

Circa 1930s, $1-3

This bridge is a favorite place for visitors to rest in Magnolia Gardens. From here a good portion of the garden can be seen mirrored on the surface of the lake.

Cancelled 1952, $2-4

C.T. 17—Beauty Spot, Magnolia Gardens, near Charleston, S. C.
"America's Most Historic City"

Magnolia Gardens, Charleston, S. C.

Visitors pause to take a few azaleas to remember a visit to Magnolia Gardens.

Cancelled 1908, $1-3

11537. ASHLEY HALL, MAGNOLIA-ON-THE-ASHLEY, CHARLESTON, S.C.

COPYRIGHT, 1907, BY
DETROIT PUBLISHING CO.

Originally, Magnolia Gardens were part of a plantation owned by the Drayton family. The current manor house is the third one to occupy the spot since the second house was burned by Union troops at the end of the Civil War.

Circa 1900s, $3-5

Before it became a public garden, Middleton Place was a working plantation. A few buildings like the old rice mill, pictured here, still survive.

Circa 1930s, $2-4

114

The river side view of the one remaining
dependency that flanked the original big house.

Circa 1930s, $3-5

The garden layout at Middleton Place was largely the work of rice plantation owner Henry
Middleton. His grandson, also named Henry, was responsible for introducing the majority
of the garden's plant life.

Circa 1930s, $1-3

The land side view of the remaining dependency. It is now a museum filled with original
Middleton furnishings.

Cancelled 1955, $3-5

The Great Oak in Middleton Place
Garden marks an old Indian trail that
ran through the site in the days before
English settlers came to Charleston.

Circa 1930s, $1-3

A number of garden paths like the one pictured here are laid out along one of the
garden's axis, which give the Middleton Place Garden an overall geometric layout.

Circa 1930s, $1-3

The reflecting pools at Middleton Place Gardens.
Supposedly it took one hundred slaves ten years
to complete the garden's layout.

Circa 1930s, $1-3

Some parts of Middleton Place Garden like, the Rice Mill Pond, were part of a working plantation.

Circa 1930s, $1-3

A canoe trip underneath the boughs of the cypress trees is a must for any visit to Cypress Gardens.

Cancelled 1931, $1-3

A reflecting pool in Middleton Place mirrors the azaleas, camellias, and live oaks planted around its edge.

Circa 1940s, $1-3

A section of Middleton Place Gardens planted along the banks of the Ashley River. After the Civil War, Middleton Place fell into disrepair but was reopened as a public garden in the 1920s.

Circa 1930s, $1-3

A rustic wooden bridge links two halves of the Cypress Garden Trail.

Circa 1930s, $2-4

The azaleas in the Yeamans Hall Club Gardens. Azaleas were introduced to South Carolina by the French botanist Andrè Michaux in the late eighteenth century.

Cancelled 1949, $2-4

Like many of the public gardens in the Charleston area, Cypress Gardens was once a privately owned plantation.

Circa 1930s, $1-3

The swampy land around Charleston is a perfect environment for growing cypress trees and they flourish in places like Cypress Gardens.

Circa 1930s, $2-4

Beaches

Part of Charleston's attraction, as with any other seaside town, are the beaches located around the city. A number of the islands in Charleston Harbor provided refuge to residents, who came to escape the heat, hectic pace, and occasional malaria outbreaks that plagued Charleston in the summer months. Developers saw the value of these beach-front communities and began buying up the surrounding land. Along with more summer homes came hotels for weekend visitors, pavilions, amusements, and boat docks for bass fishing. The construction of bridges across the Ashley and Cooper Rivers made the beaches more accessible from Charleston and reduced the travel time, which further increased the popularity of places like the Isle of Palms and Folly Beach.

Located nine miles from Charleston, the Isle of Palms is an ideal place for beach bathing because it is so close to the city and said to be free of undertow.

Circa 1940s, $4-6

The pavilion at the Isle of Palms.

Circa 1910s, $5-7

The Pavilion, Isle of Palms, Charleston, S. C.

A group of bathers relax on the beach in front of the Isle of Palms Pavilion.

Circa 1900s, $9-11

ISLE OF PALMS, CHARLESTON, S. C.—27

Eight miles long and several hundred yards wide, the Isle of Palms is Charleston's oldest and some say most desirable beach.

Circa 1930s, $7-9

Seine at Isle of Palms, Charleston, S. C.

A crowd of beach goers watch as a seine is drawn up on the beach. A seine is a vertical net that is anchored at the bottom with weights and floats along the top of the water.

Circa 1900s, $5-7

The palmettos that gave the Isle of Palms its name and Charleston the nickname "The Palmetto City."

Circa 1920s, $2-4

A mother and daughter take a break from beachcombing and sit in the shade underneath one of the palmettos that grow in profusion on the Isle of Palms.

Cancelled 1908, $4-6

In addition to being Charleston's oldest beach, the Isle of Palms was also one of the most popular, drawing tourists and residents to its shores.

Circa 1920s, $5-7

Beach at Isle of Palms, Charleston, S. C.—30

Besides bathing, the Isle of Palms also featured a variety of amusements and was well-known for bass and trout fishing.

Circa 1920s, $5-7

Palmettos grow very well in sandy soil and as a result flourished on the Isle of Palms and around Charleston.

Circa 1910s, $2-4

COPYRIGHT, 1901, BY DETROIT PHOTOGRAPHIC CO.

5777. PALMETTOES ON ISLE OF PALMS, CHARLESTON, S. C.

A Sunday afternoon crowd gathers to enjoy the sun and the surf on Folly Beach.

Circa 1930s, $4-6

Because of its location at the junction of two rivers and the edge of a large natural harbor, there were a number of beaches around the city of Charleston.

Cancelled 1925, $6-8

Folly Beach, "one of the widest and safest beaches to be found on the Atlantic Ocean." Because of the constant "tempered ocean breezes," Folly Beach also had a reputation as an excellent health resort.

Circa 1930s, $6-8

Arts & Culture

The arts were particularly popular among the "Palmetto City's" elite and as a result Charleston can lay claim to a number of cultural "firsts." Charleston was home to the first legitimate theatre in America, located on Queen Street (now the Dock Street Theatre) as well as the first paid orchestra in the English colonies sponsored by the St. Cecilia Society. Charleston was also home to Charles Theodore Pachelbell, the son of renowned composer Johann Pachelbell, one of the first European composers to emigrate to the American colonies and one of the city's most important musical figures. Private and public concerts were frequent occurrences and musicians and singers often advertised their services as performers and tutors in local newspapers and broadsheets.

Intellectual pursuits were also highly valued and interest in the study of nature and natural phenomenon resulted in the founding of the Charleston Museum in 1773, which was the first museum in this country.

Dock Street Theatre. Opened in 1736. Charleston, S. C.

Opened in 1736, the Dock Street Theater was the first legitimate theater in America.

Circa 1940s, $5-7

Dock Street Theatre and St. Phillip's Church, Charleston, S. C.

The first play performed in the theater was *The Recruiting Officer* by George Farquhar, presented on February 23, 1736.

Cancelled 1958, $5-7

C. T. 8—Historic Dock Street Theatre, Charleston, S. C.

In 1809, the Dock Street Theatre became the Planters Hotel. It was the first hotel in Charleston where the Charleston Society met.

Circa 1940s, $6-8

FOOTLIGHT PLAYERS WORKSHOP

after an etching by Alfred Hutty

Built in 1840 as a cotton warehouse, this building on Queen Street was converted into a playhouse in 1941 by the Footlight Players, the oldest community theatre group in Charleston.

Circa 1940s, $6-8

CHARLESTON MUSEUM, CHARLESTON, S. C. — 40

In response to the fervent curiosity of Charlestonians regarding natural phenomenon and the natural world, the Charleston Museum was founded in 1773.

Circa 1930s, $4-6

CHARLESTON MUSEUM, CHARLESTON, S. C.

Besides the quality of its collections, the Charleston Museum is also well-known for its cooperation with members of the local educational community.

Circa 1920s, $6-8

JAMES S. GIBBES MEMORIAL ART GALLERY, CHARLESTON, S. C.

The James B. Gibbes Memorial Art Gallery exhibits some of the finest works of art found in the state and in the county.

Cancelled 1919, $6-8

CHARLESTON MUSEUM, CHARLESTON, S. C.—52

The Charleston Museum is the oldest museum in North America. It houses a splendid collection of natural history specimens and objects from the surrounding Low Country.

Circa 1930s, $5-7

Bibliography

"Magnolia Plantation's Historical Notes of Interest." Magnolia Plantation &
Its Gardens. http://www.magnoliaplantation.com/history/index.html. 11/
23/05.

"Market Hall and Sheds." Historic Charleston's Religious and Community
Buildings. http://www.cr.nps.gov/nr/travel/charleston/mrk.htm. 11/21/05.

"Porter Military Academy." Historic Charleston's Religious and Community
Buildings. http://www.cr.nps.gov/nr/travel/charleston/por.htm. 11/21/05.

Rosen, Robert N. *Confederate Charleston: An Illustrated History of the City
and People During the Civil War*. Columbia: University of South Carolina Press, 1994.

Sully, Susan. *Charleston Style: Past and Present*. New York: Rizzoli International Publications, Inc., 1999.

"William Enston Home." Historic Charleston's Religious and Community
Buildings. http://www.cr.nps.gov/nr/travel/charleston/ens.htm. 11/21/05.

Wright, Louis B. *South Carolina: A Bicentennial History*. New York: W.W.
Norton & Company, Inc., 1976.